TRINIDAD
AND
◄ TOBAGO ►

MAJOR WORLD NATIONS

TRINIDAD AND TOBAGO

Patricia R. Urosevich

CHELSEA HOUSE PUBLISHERS
Philadelphia

Chelsea House Publishers
Contributing Author: Derek Davis

http://www.chelseahouse.com

4 5 7 9 8 6 3.

Library of Congress Cataloging-in-Publication Data
Urosevich, Patricia R.
Trinidad and Tobago / Patricia R. Urosevich
p.   cm.—(Major world nations)
Included index.
Summary: Surveys the history, topography, people, and culture of
Trinidad/Tobago, with emphasis on its current economy,
industry, and place in the political world.
ISBN 0-7910-4769-5 (hardcover)
1. Trinidad and Tobago—Juvenile literature.
[1. Trinidad and Tobago.]
I. Title. II. Series
F2119.U76   1997
972.983—dc21   97-22095
CIP
AC

◄ CONTENTS ►

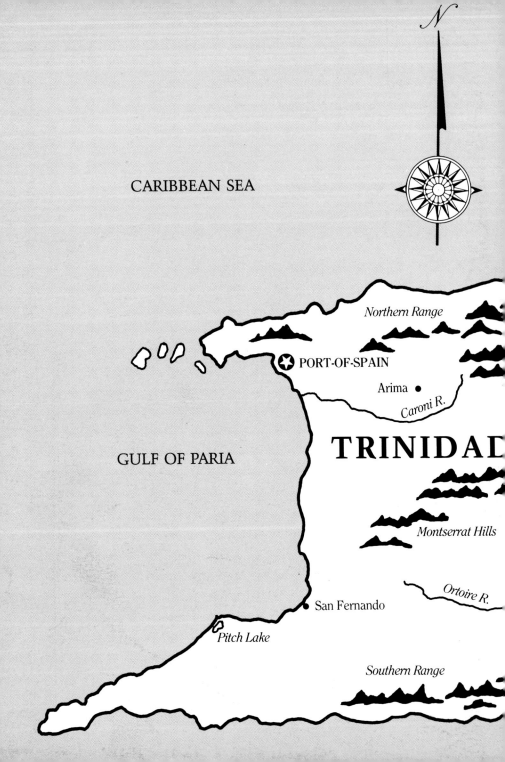

TOBAGO

LITTLE
TOBAGO

Scarborough

ATLANTIC OCEAN

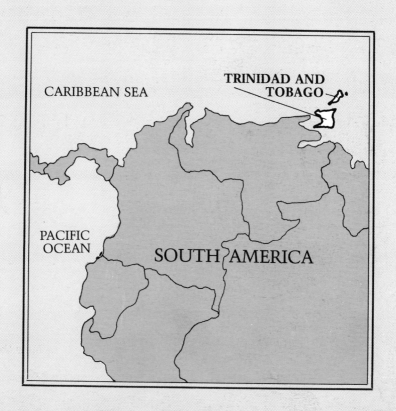

CARIBBEAN SEA

TRINIDAD AND
TOBAGO

PACIFIC
OCEAN

SOUTH AMERICA

nity
lls

◄ FACTS AT A GLANCE ►

Land and People

Location	Trinidad: approximately 7 miles (11 kilometers) east of Venezuela; Tobago: 21 miles (34 km) northeast of Trinidad
Area	1,980 square miles (5,148 square kilometers)
Highest Point	Cerro del Aripo, 3,085 feet (926 meters)
Major Lake	Pitch Lake, the world's largest natural asphalt lake
Climate	64° Fahrenheit (18° Centigrade) to 92° F (33° C); average: 78° F (26° C)
Average Annual Rainfall	80 inches (2,032 millimeters)
Capital	Port-of-Spain (population 53,000)
Population	1,300,000
Population Density	657 people per square mile (254 per sq km)
Population Distribution	Rural, 35 percent; urban, 65 percent
Official Language	English
Other Languages	Hindi, French, Spanish
Literacy Rate	97 percent
Ethnic Groups	Black, 43 percent; East Indian, 40 percent; other and mixed, 17 percent

Religions	Roman Catholic, 32 percent; Protestant, 28 percent; Hindu, 25 percent; Islam, 6 percent; other, 9 percent
Average Life Expectancy	Male, 68 years; female, 73 years
Birth Rate	16/1,000 population
Death Rate	7/1,000 population
Infant Mortality	18/1,000 live births

Economy

Major Resources	Petroleum, natural gas, lumber, fish, asphalt
Major Products	Petroleum, asphalt, ammonia, sugar
Gross Domestic Product	Equivalent to U.S. $5.4 billion
Percentage of Gross Domestic Product:	Services, 28 percent; petroleum and natural gas, 27 percent; finance, insurance, and real estate, 13 percent; government, 10 percent; manufacturing, 9 percent; agriculture, 3 percent; other, 10 percent
Currency	Trinidad and Tobago dollar

Government

Form of Government	Bicameral democracy, with an appointed 31-member Senate and an elected 36-member House of Representatives
Formal Head of State	President
Head of Government	Prime Minister
Eligibility to Vote	All adults age 18 or over

◄HISTORY AT A GLANCE►

10,000 B.C.	The islands of Trinidad and Tobago tear away from the South American continent.
5000 B.C.	Arawak and Carib Indians migrate to the islands.
1498 A.D.	Columbus sights and names Trinidad, claiming it for Spain.
1532	The first Spanish settlers arrive on Trinidad.
1608	Britain claims Tobago.
1632	Dutch colonists establish the first permanent settlement on Tobago.
1702	The first African slaves arrive on Trinidad.
1762 to 1814	France, Spain, Britain, and Holland fight over Tobago. The island changes hands 31 times.
1783	Spain offers land grants on Trinidad to any Roman Catholic from Spain or an allied nation. Many French planters accept the offer.
1797	Britain attacks and captures Trinidad.
1802	The Treaty of Amiens gives Trinidad to England, ending Spain's 300-year rule. France gets Tobago.
1814	Britain wins final control of Tobago.
1834	Britain abolishes slavery in all of its colonies.
1844	Britain institutes a program to bring indentured servants from India to Trinidad. Many remain on the island after their terms of service have ended.

1889   Tobago's sugar industry collapses and Britain combines Trinidad and Tobago into a single colony.

1908   Trinidad sinks its first oil well.

1940   Britain exchanges a lease to a United States naval base on Trinidad for war supplies. Although the action boosts the economy, islanders resent being given no voice in the agreement.

1946   All adults are granted the right to vote.

1956   Trinidad and Tobago obtain limited self-government.

1960   The United States agrees to abandon its naval base by 1977.

1962   Trinidad and Tobago becomes independent within the Commonwealth of Nations.

1971   High unemployment leads to riots and brief army mutiny.

1976   Trinidad and Tobago becomes a republic, with an elected president replacing the queen of England as head of state.

1990   Muslim extremists capture the Parliament building and hold about 50 hostages, including the prime minister, before surrendering after a siege of several days.

1995   Basdeo Panday becomes the country's first prime minister of East Indian heritage.

1997   Arthur Napoleon Raymond Robinson is elected president.

2001   President Robinson faces possible impeachment by refusing to swear in seven cabinet members who lost December parliamentary elections.

TRINIDAD
AND
❮ TOBAGO ❯

Cannons peer out to sea from Fort James, Trinidad. Many forts were built during the 17th and 18th centuries to protect the strategically located islands from attack.

Trinidad and Tobago and the World

The nation of Trinidad and Tobago consists of two small islands in the Caribbean Sea, at the southernmost end of the West Indian island chain. Despite its Caribbean location, however, the country's land, economy, and ethnic mix differ greatly from those of its island neighbors. Geography and history have made these islands unique.

In prehistoric times, Trinidad and Tobago were part of South America. Scientists believe that the islands separated from the continent about 10,000 years ago. Physically, then, Trinidad and Tobago are linked to the South American continent. But historically and culturally, the islands have been influenced by Europe, Asia, and Africa. Christopher Columbus discovered Trinidad in 1498, beginning an era of Spanish colonization. Soon afterward, other European powers vied for control of the islands, and British and Dutch settlers established communities on both islands. In the 18th century, these colonists began importing African slaves to the islands, adding yet another ethnic influence.

In the late 18th century, French planters arrived on Trinidad. By the mid-19th century, after slavery had been abolished, servants from India were imported to labor on colonial plantations. Various other Europeans and Middle Easterners arrived over the years, making Trinidad and Tobago one of the most ethnically diverse nations in the world.

The nation's 1.3 million people have managed to blend their many influences into a unique and vibrant culture. The racial violence that other ethnically mixed countries have experienced has generally not plagued Trinidad and Tobago. Rather, the cultural blending has created unique traditions that have become popular throughout the world. Almost everyone is familiar with calypso music and steel-drum bands, both of which originated in Trinidad and Tobago.

The islands' political influences are largely British. Great Britain gained control of Trinidad and Tobago in the 19th century and combined them into one nation in 1889. Although the islands became an independent republic in 1976, they still retain strong ties to Great Britain, and their government is based primarily on the British system.

Trinidad and Tobago's ports now ship more in exports than they receive in imports.

During the years of colonization, Trinidad and Tobago's economy was rooted in agriculture, and farm products such as sugar and cocoa are still vital sources of revenue. But the country has other natural resources besides its fertile soil. Oil fields, natural gas, and the world's largest pitch lake (a natural tar reservoir) all contribute to Trinidad and Tobago's modern, industrialized economy. The nation trades with countries around the world, importing crude oil from the Middle East and exporting urea (a natural compound used to make resins and plastics) to the United States, the Netherlands, and India. Since the 1970s, Trinidad and Tobago has maintained a favorable balance of trade, selling more to other nations than it buys from them.

Increased dependence on oil production led to an economic boom in the 1970s, followed by a long recession in the 1980s and early 1990s as oil prices fell. Also, the great number of state-owned companies tended to discourage other countries and private companies from investing in Trinidad and Tobago. In recent years, however, the government has sold many industries to private corporations and has changed its tax and tariff structure to encourage outside investment. The recession has lifted, and the country now boasts extensive financial services, such as banking.

On the negative side, unemployment has remained near 20 percent for many years, and there is some concern that too many industries are now dominated by United States and British companies. However, over the long run, the North American Free Trade Agreement (NAFTA) is expected to increase trade greatly between the United States and all Caribbean nations. On balance, Trinidad and Tobago's prospects for the 21st century look bright.

*King's Bay waterfall on Tobago is one of the country's many spectacular land features.
Others include the Trinity Hills, from which Trinidad takes its name.*

Mountains, Valleys, and Beaches

Situated in the Caribbean Sea only a few miles (kilometers) off the South American coast, Trinidad and Tobago consists of two large islands surrounded by many smaller islands and cays (small islands or reefs made of sand or coral). Taken together, the islands have an area of 1,980 square miles (5,148 square kilometers), making the entire nation about the same size as the state of Delaware.

Trinidad, the largest island, lies approximately 7 miles (11 kilometers) east of Venezuela. It is bounded by the Gulf of Paria in the west, the Caribbean Sea in the north, the Atlantic Ocean in the east, and the Columbus Channel in the south. About 50 miles (81 km) long and 70 miles (113 km) wide, Trinidad has an area of 1,864 square miles (4,846 sq km). Its shape has been compared to that of a conquistador's boot.

Three mountain ranges run from east to west across Trinidad. The rugged Northern Range, which was part of the South American Andes before the island broke away from the continent, is covered with thick, green timber. It includes Cerro del Aripo, the highest peak in the country at 3,085 feet (926 meters). The Montserrat Hills cut across the island's center, and the Southern Range lines the lower coast. In the island's southeastern corner, three rugged peaks known as the Trinity Hills peer over the sea. Columbus named the island after these hills.

Trinidad is a land of mountains. Three ranges—the Northern Range, the Montserrat Hills, and the Southern Range—span the tiny island.

Hilly plains and fertile valleys separate the island's mountain ranges. Thick forests, grasslands, and swamps cover the southern end of the island, which is also the site of the world's largest pitch lake (a lake containing tar). This fertile area produces most of the island's sugarcane, and the valleys produce a wide variety of tropical crops.

Trinidad has many rivers and streams. The two largest are the Caroni in the north, which flows westward to the Caribbean Sea, and the Ortoire in the south, which flows eastward into the Atlantic Ocean. Smaller rivers include the Poole River (a tributary of the Ortoire) and the Oropuche. None of these rivers is navigable.

Tobago

Located about 21 miles (34 kilometers) northeast of Trinidad, Tobago is known for its tranquility and beach-lined coasts. Shaped like a cigar, it is 27 miles (43 km) long and 7 miles (11 km) wide. Its surface area of 116 square miles (302 square kilometers) makes it almost 16 times smaller than Trinidad. Tobago is bordered by the Atlantic Ocean to the south and east and by the Caribbean to the north and west.

A chain of volcanic hills runs the length of the island. Thickly covered with trees, the hills slope to a narrow plain in the south. Pigeon Point, along the northeast coast, rises to a height of 1,800 feet (540 kilometers), the island's highest peak. Fertile valleys run inland from the coast and are the site of sugar, coconut, and pineapple plantations. King's Bay waterfall, on the island's east coast, plunges 110 feet (33 meters), making it the highest falls in the country.

Tobago greatly resembles the beautiful island paradise that British author Daniel Defoe described in his novel *Robinson Crusoe*. The similarity may be more than a coincidence. A site on the island's southwest coast, now known as Robinson Crusoe's cave, is said to have inspired the novel's setting.

Tobago has become a haven for tourists from Europe, the Americas, and Trinidad.

Sixteen small islands and cays are scattered in the waters surrounding Trinidad and Tobago. The largest of these, Little Tobago (also known as Bird of Paradise Island), is located off Tobago's east coast. A number of smaller islands are situated off Trinidad's northwest coast, in a channel known as Dragon's Mouth. These include Chacachacare, Huevos, Monos, and Gaspar Grande.

Tropical Breezes

Trinidad and Tobago is a tropical country, because it is south of the Tropic of Cancer, the latitude line considered the boundary between the tropics and the temperate middle zone of the north. Northeast trade winds blow across the islands year-round, keeping the temperatures mild and the humidity moderate. Normally, temperatures on the islands average a high of between 80° to 84° Fahrenheit (27° to 29° Centigrade) during the day and fall to about 75° F (24° C) at night. Because of its location, Tobago is slightly cooler and less humid than Trinidad.

The islands have definite rainy and dry seasons. The rainy season, which extends from June to December, brings an average yearly rainfall of 70 inches (1,778 millimeters). During these months, it rains heavily for a few hours each day. A short dry spell, known as "Petit Carême," occurs during September and October. From January through May, the islands are usually warm and dry. Although a few storms have hit Trinidad and Tobago during its history, hurricanes are rare because the islands lie south of the Caribbean hurricane belt.

A Wildlife Paradise

Geologists believe that Trinidad and Tobago tore away from the South American continent about 10,000 B.C., when shifts in the earth's plates sent the islands out into the sea. Its geological link to South America has made Trinidad and Tobago home to more varieties of plant and animal life than its Caribbean neighbors. More than 400 kinds of birds, 55 reptiles, 97 mammals, and 25 amphibians inhabit this island nation.

Trinidad and Tobago has more tropical birds per acre (hectare) than any other Caribbean island. Along Trinidad's north coast, scores of honey-creepers, swallow-tailed kites, and black hawks thrive. Several varieties of birds are found only on the islands. The paui, for example, lives only on Trinidad. It resembles a turkey and was once considered a gourmet delicacy (it is now an endangered species). Many rare herons—most notably the agami, the chestnut-bellied, and the boat-bellied—also nest along Trinidad's coast and in its swamps. The world's only ramphasite toucans are found in Trinidad's forests, and Little Tobago is the only place in the world outside of New Guinea where birds of paradise fly freely. The birds are not native to the area, however; they were brought to the island in 1909.

Trinidad was once called the "Land of the Hummingbird" because more than 19 varieties of the bird live there. Tobago is home to 7 varieties

Trinidad and Tobago is home to more than a dozen varieties of hummingbirds.

of hummingbirds. But the national bird is the colorful scarlet ibis. The Caroni Bird Sanctuary outside of Port-of-Spain on Trinidad has many of these beautiful birds, and both islands have many outdoor bird-watching areas.

In addition to birds, rare butterflies also color the islands' skies. The hillsides surrounding Port-of-Spain are home to the rare *Diathria aurelia*. Other common species include the tiger, king page, d'abricot, and emperor butterflies. But by far the most prolific flying creature in Trinidad and Tobago is the bat. In fact, Trinidad has the densest bat population in the world. Approximately 60 varieties, ranging in size from those with a 4-inch (10-centimeter) wingspan to those with leathery wings stretching more than 3 feet (.9 meter), inhabit the islands.

In addition to bats, the islands boast 96 other species of mammals, including monkeys, deer, wild hogs, opossums, raccoons, rodents, ocelots, and armadillos. Reptiles include the caiman, a type of crocodile. More than 300 varieties of tropical fish can be seen swimming in the clear waters surrounding the islands. The most notable are the kingfish, which reaches a length of 6 feet (1.8 meters) and can weigh up to 80 pounds (36 kilograms), and the queen angelfish, one of the Caribbean's most colorful species.

Wildflowers, trees, shrubs, and other plants grow everywhere in Trinidad and Tobago. Its warm climate and heavy rains nourish a variety of tropical plants. In addition to this natural vegetation, formal, European-style gardens have been planted throughout the islands, displaying a palette of color. Working plantations overflow with precise rows of cacao plants and colorful tropical fruits.

Thousands of varieties of flowers and flowering trees bloom on Trinidad and Tobago. More than 700 species of orchids alone blanket the islands. In fact, the islanders mark their seasons by noting the flowers and trees that are blooming. In March and April, the poui tree's pink and yellow flowers signal spring. The golden blossoms that illuminate the sassia fistula tree in May or June mark the end of the dry season. The bright

Warm ocean breezes and abundant rains nurture tropical fruits, including mangoes.

red blossoms of the flamboyant and immortelle, two of the islands' most striking flowering trees, herald fall's arrival, and the wild poinsettia (the national flower) marks winter.

Both Trinidad and Tobago have thick timber forests that contain many commercial lumber trees. Mahogany and cedar grow throughout the islands, and pine and teak plantations have recently been established in the eastern part of Trinidad. The land, with its beauty and variety of natural resources, has long been one of the nation's greatest assets. The government hopes to use these assets to bring more tourists and businesses to the islands.

On his third voyage to the New World, Columbus sighted Trinidad, named it, and claimed it for Spain. The Spanish were disappointed that the island had no gold.

A Colonial Past

Along with the rest of the Caribbean region, Trinidad and Tobago experienced a long period of European colonization. The islands' first inhabitants were the Arawak and Carib Indians who migrated to the islands from South America as early as 5000 B.C. The cannibalistic Caribs lived primarily on Tobago, while Trinidad was populated by the peaceful Arawaks. Although the Caribs stalked the Arawaks and dominated many West Indian islands, life in Trinidad and Tobago was relatively peaceful until 1498, when Christopher Columbus spotted Trinidad on his third voyage to the New World.

Columbus named the island he discovered "La Trinidad" (The Trinity), after the three peaks on its southern coast. He said they reminded him of the Holy Trinity of Christianity (the Father, Son, and Holy Ghost). The explorer claimed the island for Spain. For some reason that remains a mystery, however, he did not record sighting Tobago, so the tiny neighboring island remained unclaimed.

The discovery of Trinidad initially excited the Spaniards, but they were quickly disappointed. First of all, the island lacked the precious metals, such as gold and silver, that had been found on other islands. Furthermore, the marauding Caribs discouraged settlement. In the 1520s, Spain discovered Mexico and Peru and found that these lands were rich in metals and other resources. As a result, Trinidad became merely a temporary stopover point for Spanish ships in need of fuel, water, and food supplies.

As other nations began to explore the Caribbean, however, Trinidad and Tobago became valuable for their strategic position. When British sea captain Lawrence Keymis discovered Tobago in 1608, he promptly claimed it for England. British colonists arrived on the island in 1616. The island's natural harbors and position on the path of the trade winds appealed to several European nations (as well as to pirates), and although the British settlers were soon driven off by the Caribs, other Europeans followed them to Tobago. Dutch settlers attempted to colonize the island in 1632, and Courtlanders from Latvia on the Baltic Sea also flocked there. The Courtlanders were the first settlers to farm tobacco, and historians believe the island got its name from the Carib word for pipe.

These European settlers threatened Spain's attempt to monopolize the New World's riches. Needing a defensive stronghold to protect their interests on the mainland, the Spaniards returned to Trinidad and tried to fortify it by encouraging Spanish colonization and tightening control of local authorities. The effort failed, however, and Spain's inability to control the island prompted a Dutch raid in 1640 and a French raid in 1690. Throughout the next century, Tobago changed hands as many as 31 times as the European powers alternately attacked it and signed it away in treaties.

The Arawaks and Caribs resisted European settlement, and they were initially successful in driving the settlers away. But as more colonists arrived, the outnumbered Indians lost ground. The Europeans used sophisticated weapons to subdue the Indians. They sent many to work as slaves on other islands or put them to work on plantations on Trinidad and Tobago, where overwork and disease soon took their toll. By the end of the 17th century, few of the original inhabitants were left on the islands.

By the 18th century, the Europeans had created a thriving sugar industry in the West Indies, and Trinidad and Tobago's fertile soil attracted many people. Settlers came from all over Europe, bringing with them African slaves to work their fields. The islands became profitable agricultural centers. Tobago's plantations were particularly successful.

This success began to worry Spain. It feared that Trinidad's inhabitants—who now included people from all over Europe—were not loyal to Spanish interests. In 1783, it offered land grants and tax exemptions to lure Roman Catholics from any of its allied countries to Trinidad. The deal attracted French colonists from Haiti (a colony on the island of Hispaniola in the northern Caribbean), where slavery had been abolished. Hundreds of French planters and their black slaves migrated to Trinidad. But instead of bringing in people who would be loyal to Spain, the action added large numbers of French and Africans to Trinidad's growing potpourri. So many French settlers came to the island that, by the end of the century, Trinidad was more French than Spanish.

Meanwhile, conflicts among the various European powers continued to rage, and in 1797, Britain invaded Trinidad at Port-of-Spain. The weak island government surrendered before a shot was fired, and in 1802, Spain legally awarded Trinidad to Britain under the Treaty of Amiens. Almost 300 years of Spanish control had come to an end.

The Treaty of Amiens also awarded Tobago to France. But the battle for the tiny island was not over. In 1803, Britain and France went to war

After the British reclaimed Trinidad and Tobago, they installed James Woodford as the territory's first governor.

again, and by 1810, the British had captured almost every French, Dutch, and Danish territory in the West Indies. In 1814, the British reclaimed Tobago. They would keep it for the next 150 years.

Raising the Union Jack

British control of Trinidad and Tobago did not drastically alter island life. The islands' economy continued to depend on agriculture—particularly sugarcane, grown on plantations worked by slaves. But in 1834, the British government outlawed slavery, and most slaves fled the plantations. Some migrated to other islands, others purchased small tracts of land to become independent farmers, and still others worked part-time on their own land and only occasionally on plantations for wages. As a result, the plantation owners were faced with a serious labor shortage.

Deprived of their labor force and faced with stiff competition in the sugar market, the British frantically searched for ways to save their sugar industry. In 1845, they initiated an indentured servant program that would once again change the country's ethnic makeup. Under this program, workers from overpopulated India (and later China) would work on Trinidad's plantations for five years and then receive passage home. Although some workers did return to Asia after their term ended, many stayed in Trinidad. By the time the program ended in 1917, almost one-third of the island's population was East Indian.

But competition in the sugar market continued to grow, and, despite this new labor force, the British company that marketed Tobago's sugar eventually went bankrupt. The island's industry collapsed, taking the entire Tobagoan economy with it. In 1889, the British government decided it was too expensive to administer Trinidad and Tobago separately. Without consulting the islanders, it combined the two into a single colony.

Consolidated rule did not change the islands' financial situation, however, and the islanders began looking in new directions for economic stability. Inhabitants of Tobago diversified their crops and found another use for their island's natural beauty—they began to develop a tourism industry.

In 1908, Trinidad began to develop its oil resources. The economy revived. But the next few decades again brought economic turmoil, and the 1930s ushered in the Great Depression, a worldwide economic crisis that sent millions of people into poverty.

Trinidad and Tobago suffered greatly during the depression. Between 1934 and 1938, the oilfields became the scene of strikes and riots as workers appealed for higher wages and protested discrimination by their European employers. In the late 1930s, an islander named Uriah Butler helped to organize a large general union for thousands of unskilled workers. The workers' movement became a powerful force in island politics that grew

Slaves worked the islands' profitable sugar plantations until 1834, when slavery was outlawed. The slaves fled the plantations and were replaced by Indian servants.

Roosevelt (left) and Churchill upset islanders by striking a land deal.

into political parties in the 1950s. Nevertheless, the movement's efforts could not erase the depression that continued to affect the islanders until World War II revived the economy.

In the summer of 1940, as war raged in Europe, British prime minister Winston Churchill and United States president Franklin Roosevelt struck a controversial deal that rekindled the islands' economy. The British swapped a 99-year lease on a large tract of land on Trinidad for ships and rifles that they needed for their World War II effort. The United States established a naval base on the land. Although the base brought many jobs, the islanders were upset that Britain could give away their land without even consulting them.

Moving toward Independence

After World War II, European colonies all over the world began demanding more participation in government affairs. Trinidad and Tobago was no exception. In the late 1940s, Britain was forced to decrease its control over Trinidad and Tobago's government. In 1946, it granted all adult islanders the right to vote. By the 1950s, the islanders began forming political parties. The strongest of these was the People's National movement (PNM), led by Dr. Eric Williams. The party quickly became a powerful force in island politics. In 1956, the British government granted Trinidad and Tobago limited self-government and installed Williams as chief minister.

With Williams at the helm, the islands quickly began moving toward independence. In 1960, for example, the government scored its first international diplomatic victory when it negotiated the end of the U.S. naval base lease, persuading the United States to surrender the land in 1977.

On August 31, 1962, Trinidad and Tobago became an independent member of the Commonwealth of Nations (a political and economic organization made up of former British colonies). This new status meant that, although the British monarch remained the formal head of state, a new government, with a prime minister as its leader, was declared. Williams was selected as the islands' first prime minister.

Dr. Williams led the PNM and became the islands' first prime minister.

The new government worked to improve education and fight poverty and unemployment. To strengthen economic ties with its neighbors, Trinidad and Tobago joined the Caribbean Free Trade Area in 1968 and the Caribbean Common Market in 1973. (Both organizations work to promote economic cooperation among Caribbean nations.) Despite accomplishments in education and health, however, high unemployment continued to plague the nation.

In the early 1970s, black power advocates vehemently protested the unemployment rate, as well as social and economic inequality throughout the islands. The protests soon led to widespread riots and, in April 1970, an army mutiny. Williams was forced to declare a temporary state of emergency, but order was quickly restored with the help of United States soldiers stationed on the island.

When black activists demanded social equality in 1970, riots rocked the islands.

Many islanders objected to Williams's handling of the unrest. In protest, the nation's opposition parties boycotted the election of May 1971. This tactic backfired, however. With only 32 percent of the electorate voting, Williams's PNM party won every seat in the House of Representatives.

Although the high unemployment rate persisted, the sudden rise of oil prices in 1973 and 1974 pumped new life into the nation's sagging economy. Huge oil earnings gave the government the money needed to lower taxes, increase welfare benefits, control the prices of food staples, and increase industrial investments.

The New Republic

In August 1976, a new constitution declared Trinidad and Tobago a republic within the Commonwealth of Nations. The British monarch was replaced as head of state by a president elected to a five-year term. (The islanders chose PNM member Ellis Clarke as their new president.) The prime minister remained the head of government, and Williams served in this post until his death in 1981.

When oil prices fell and the government proved still unable to repair the unemployment problems and the uneven distribution of wealth, the PNM was soundly defeated in the 1986 elections by a new party, the National Alliance for Reconstruction (NAR). After a failed Black Muslim extremist attempt to overthrow the government in 1990, the PNM returned to power. In the meantime, the country's economic recession began to ease.

The 1995 elections ended in a deadlock between the PNM and a heavily East Indian party, the United National Congress (UNC). The UNC formed an alliance with the NAR and took power under UNC prime minister Basdeo Panday. All three parties are pledged to similar goals of improving the lot of all citizens by encouraging a free-market economy and loosening government control over business operations.

Trinidad and Tobago's people come from a variety of ethnic groups whose forefathers came to the island when it was a British colony.

The People

Approximately 1.3 million people live in Trinidad and Tobago, 95 percent of them on the island of Trinidad. The majority of the islanders are quite young—the 1995 census found that 31 percent are under the age of 15. Only 35 percent live in rural areas, while the remaining 65 percent have homes in or near the country's cities.

Trinidad and Tobago has the most ethnically and culturally diverse population in the Caribbean. Its people have roots in African, Asian, and European countries and practice a variety of religions, including Roman Catholicism, Hinduism, and Islam. Forty-three percent of the people are of African descent, making this the largest ethnic group in the nation. East Indians follow closely, comprising 40 percent of the population. The rest of the islanders can trace their backgrounds to France, Spain, Great Britain, Portugal, Syria, Lebanon, China, and the Americas. There are also many Creoles (people of mixed European and African descent).

On Trinidad, Africans and East Indians favor different parts of the island. Industrially developed cities such as Port-of-Spain in the northwest, Arima in the north central area, and San Fernando in the southwest are home to most of the African and mixed populations.

Most of Trinidad's East Indians prefer to live in the agricultural areas on the island's west side. There, they practice a way of life based on the

*More than 50 percent of the islanders
have some African ancestry.*

values and beliefs of their ancestors' native India. Many Indian traditions have been preserved. For example, marriages are often arranged by the parents, and East Indian women are usually married by the age of 25. Most of Trinidad's East Indians view marriage as a permanent commitment and do not condone divorce or the remarriage of widows. However, there are signs that these traditions are being strained by the modern world. The suicide rate among young East Indian women in the mid-1990s was twice that among non–East Indian women.

Tobago's population is mostly of African descent and is more evenly distributed than Trinidad's. More than half of its people are settled in its one city, Scarborough. The rest are scattered in small towns throughout the island.

Religious Heritage

Almost two-thirds of Trinidad and Tobago's people practice Christianity. Roman Catholics are the islands' largest group, although many other islanders are Anglicans or Presbyterians. The East Indians brought with them their Hindu faith, still practiced by 25 percent of the population. Another 6 percent of the people are Muslims.

Some islanders of African descent belong to the Shango cult, a religious sect that worships Shango, the god of thunder and lightning. The Shango cult mixes African beliefs with Christianity by combining tribal

This mosque on Trinidad serves the islands' Muslims (6 percent of the population).

gods with Christian saints. Its followers have kept alive various old plantation practices, such as drum beating, midnight meetings, sacrificial offer-
ings of white cocks or pigeons, and magic. They believe that after a person
dies, his shadow or spirit remains and continues to live unless properly
dismissed. Therefore, nine days after a death, Shango followers gather
ceremoniously to put the dead person's shadow to rest.

Religion plays an important role in the lives of all the islanders, and
the government recognizes many religious events as national holidays.
Christians celebrate Christmas, Good Friday, Easter, Whitmonday (usually
in May), and Corpus Christi (also in the late spring). Diwali is celebrated in
October or November by Hindus. The Muslim Eid-ul-Fitr is recognized as
well. Other national holidays include Independence Day, Emancipation
Day, Labor Day, and Republic Day.

Two religious festivals can be enjoyed by the whole community. On
Diwali, also known as the Hindu festival of lights, devout Hindus honor the
goddess Lakshmi by placing thousands of small pottery lamps around their
homes and temples. Hosay, the Muslim festival, brings hundreds of Muslims to the streets, where they parade, sing, and display large, colorful
models of mosques.

Daily Life

The islands' main family unit is the household group. In addition to the
nuclear family—a father, mother, and their children—this group includes
grandparents, uncles and aunts, cousins, and other relatives. Both African
and East Indian families live in this manner.

Most islanders do not live as elaborately as most Europeans or Ameri-
cans do. Trinidad and Tobago suffers from a serious housing shortage. In
an attempt to supply adequate housing for low-income families, the government is building modern concrete dwellings throughout the islands.
But most private residences are small, wooden structures with galvanized
metal roofs. They usually have about four rooms, electricity, and piped-in
water. Some families, however, must still draw water from nearby wells and

(continued on page 49)

SCENES OF

TRINIDAD
AND
‹TOBAGO›

➤ Fishermen at Courland
Bay on Tobago prepare
their nets for a day's
fishing.

⌄ Man O' War Bay on the Tobagoan coast is a natural harbor for small craft.

⋏ *Scarborough, Tobago's largest town, is a small and tranquil village.*

⋏ *Although cars are plentiful, older methods of transportation are still used.*

◀ *The Central Market in Port-of-Spain attracts people from all over the islands.*

✦ Souvenir shops at island hotels sell a variety of local crafts.

◄ Cultural exhibitions celebrate the islands' many ethnic influences.

➤ The cannons that once protected Tobago from attack are now surrounded by a lovely garden.

➤ *Rolling hills surround Scarborough.*

Y *Since the early 1900s, oil has been the islands' primary industry.*

⋏ *Many homes are built on stilts to protect them from rising waters.*

◂ *The scarlet ibis, the national bird, nests at the Caroni Bird Sanctuary.*

⋏ *Both islands have many outdoor bird-watching areas.*

◄ *A load of plantains waits
at the Port-of-Spain dock.*

Ⅴ *Plush hotels combine the islands' natural beauty with modern amenities.*

➤ *During carnival, separate events and competitions are held for children.*

⋎ *At Hillsborough Bay, a narrow road parallels Tobago's palm-lined coast.*

other water sources and it is common for several houses to share a common yard.

The clothes, food, and speech of the islanders reflect their diverse backgrounds. Although the weather is warm, dress is more formal and conservative than on other West Indian islands. In Port-of-Spain, business attire is the norm. The Caribbean shirt jac, a belted jacket and scarf with no shirt, has gained popularity for men, replacing the traditional suit. Women most often wear dresses. On the farms and in the refineries, work clothes are common. Some East Indians prefer traditional clothing, such as colorful saris for women and turbans for men.

Island cooking is as diverse as the population. Each morning, the average family partakes of a "continental" breakfast of bread and coffee or cocoa. Lunch and dinner (which is not served until eight or nine P.M.) are full meals—meat, rice, a green vegetable, fruit, and a beverage are served. *Roti*, thin pancakes, are available everywhere on the islands. They are often filled with curried lamb, beef, or chicken, and sometimes cooked vegetables. Vendors sell them on the streets in the cities. Trinidad's most typical dish, *sans couche*, is a stew of pork, salted beef, pig's tail, onions, chives, and other spices. It is served with dumplings. *Accra*, Tobago's specialty, is salted fish pounded with seasonings and yeast, then shaped into small cakes and fried. It is served with fritters called "floats."

The language of the islands owes its dialects and idiosyncracies to its history. Although English is the official language, French patois, Hindustani, and Spanish are also spoken in the countryside. Dialects vary between cities, towns, and agricultural areas, and are generally considered a status index. Business people and the upper class strive for a proper British accent, while others speak with the lilt and vocabulary found in calypso music.

The British influence can also be found in recreational pastimes. The people of Trinidad and Tobago enjoy cricket and horse racing. Soccer, often called football, is a favorite among all classes. Nearly every city, town, and village has its own soccer team.

Tropical fruits are an important part of the island diet.

Cosmopolitan Culture

The islanders' varying ethnic and religious backgrounds have influenced Trinidad and Tobago's art and culture in many ways. The country is best known for its unique musical contributions to Caribbean culture: calypso and steel bands. These musical forms grew out of the islanders' desire to express themselves through music and were shaped by the lives and experiences of their creators.

The older of these native forms is calypso, a rhythmic and lively vocal style. Plantation workers created calypso as a form of entertainment. Through their music, they ridiculed the greed, envy, and vanity of the plantation owners and contrasted it with their own simple existences. Today, calypso lyrics poke fun at local politics, local figures, and society in general.

Calypsonians, the men and women who write the words and music for the songs, vary in personal style and dialect. The most famous calypsonians are as well known on the islands as Frank Sinatra and Elvis Presley are known in the United States. The all-time great calypsonians are the Mighty Sparrow (Francisco Slinger) and Lord Kitchener (Aldwyn Roberts). Other notables include the Shadow (Winston Bailey), Rose (McCartha Sandy-Lewis, one of a few women to achieve fame), and Superblue (Austin Lyons).

Calypso music thrives year-round, but it comes to a peak during carnival, the celebration that ushers in the Lenten season (the 40 days that precede Easter). About four weeks before carnival, Trinidad and Tobago's most famous calypsonians, along with others hoping to be recognized, perform their latest songs around Port-of-Spain. As many as two or three dozen perform nightly at several locations. Competitors are eliminated until eight finalists are left to compete for one of the carnival's most sought-after titles: Calypso Monarch. Calypsonians also compete for the

The steel-drum sound has roots in both African and East Indian music.

title of Road March King, awarded to the person whose tune is played the most on carnival Monday and Tuesday.

Trinidad and Tobago's other famous musical style is steel band music. The steel band sound is an infectious musical rhythm with a pounding beat and notes similar to American jazz. Steel bands developed from the ceremonial drumming of the Africans and East Indians. Many of the African slaves who arrived in Trinidad and Tobago worshipped Shango, the god of thunder and lightning, and participated in religious ceremonies requiring the use of sacred drums. From these ceremonies, the steel drum sound was born.

Today's steel band consists of four basic instruments, known collectively as pans: the boom, the cello pan, the guitar pan, and the ping-pong. All are made from empty oil drums with the bottoms cut off. Craftsmen hammer the top into a convex shape, then use a small sledge hammer and chisel to create the indentations that make the notes.

Steel bands also compete during carnival. Every year, one steel band is honored as best steel band of the carnival. To achieve this title, bands throughout the nation participate in the Panorama Championship Competition, two qualifying rounds held before the official beginning of carnival.

Carnival

Historians believe that Trinidad and Tobago's first carnival was held in about 1783. Carnival derived from the French custom of holding a party season from Christmas to Ash Wednesday, the first day of Lent. Throughout the party season, groups of masked and disguised individuals paraded through the streets, sometimes with musical accompaniment. After the slaves were emancipated in 1834, the carnival grew in size as parties once held in private ballrooms spilled out into the streets.

Today, the carnival officially kicks off two days before Ash Wednesday, but preparations begin long before then. Port-of-Spain starts buzzing about a week before Ash Wednesday. Groups, known as bands, some with more than 5,000 masqueraders, divide into several differently costumed

During carnival, masqueraders parade through the streets in lavish costumes.

groups. Each group's costume portrays an element in the overall theme created by the "mas" leader. Themes are usually based on fantasy, history, religion, or politics.

The Sunday before Ash Wednesday, known as Dimanche Gras, is marked by three noteworthy competitions: Calypso Monarch, Carnival King, and Carnival Queen. The Calypso Monarch is selected on the basis of his or her music, while the king and queen win for their costumes. When the Dimanche Gras show ends, people join in public and private parties. At dawn on Carnival Monday, the revelers spill into the streets, where they dance to carnival music played by steel and brass bands. That afternoon, they hold a parade.

Monday's festivities are only a warm-up for Tuesday's events. Early on Carnival Tuesday, the costumed bands begin lining up along the parade route, which winds though the streets of Port-of-Spain to Queens Park Savannah. At Queen's Park, they cross the stage for the judging of the carnival's best band, the most heralded event of the carnival.

The celebration continues into the night. This "las lap" offers one last chance to jump in the streets before the year's carnival celebration ends at midnight. The next day is Ash Wednesday, which marks the beginning of Lent, a period of prayer and fasting for devout Christians.

Other Cultural Outlets

In addition to carnival and its events, Trinidad and Tobago hosts a steel band festival and a national music festival of arts. The annual Best Village Trophy competition in music, handicrafts, fine arts, and performing arts has spawned an avid interest in folk theater. During the performing arts competition, hundreds of villages throughout the nation perform in one-act plays.

Trinidad and Tobago also has several professional theater groups that mount local stage productions. Known for its dramatic diversity, the Little Carib Theatre books productions by a variety of theatrical groups. Some of the theater companies, such as the Trinidad Theatre Workshop, have been active for many years.

Literature

Trinidad and Tobago did not develop its own literature until the 20th century, but some of its writers have achieved international acclaim. Many island works center on the themes of social and ethnic identity in Trinidad and Tobago's cultural potpourri. An example is E. A. Mittelholzer's *Morning at the Office*, which described how the nation's race and color dif-

Crowds pack Queen's Park Savannah in Port-of-Spain each year at carnival time.

ferences created friction between people. Some East Indian novelists, such as Ismith Khan and V.S. Naipaul, left the islands to live elsewhere, but drew characters and situations from their West Indian upbringing. Derek Walcott, a poet who won the Nobel Prize in 1992, lived on Trinidad for years.

Locally produced art reflects the ethnic and cultural diversity of Trinidad and Tobago's population. It can be viewed informally at many of the nation's shops and open-air markets, or more ceremoniously at the National Museum and Art Gallery in Port-of-Spain. Some of the best examples of island crafts include wood carvings, hand-beaten copper jewelry, woven straw items, steel band drums, and boldly printed fabrics.

Basdeo Panday, Trinidad and Tobago's first prime minister of East Indian origin, was elected to office in 1995.

Government:
A British Heritage

Political and economic stability are the hallmarks of Trinidad and Tobago's democratic government. As it moved peacefully from a British colony to an independent nation, it adopted many of Britain's governmental and legal systems. Like Great Britain, Trinidad and Tobago has a two-chambered Parliament. The Parliament consists of a Senate and House of Representatives led by the prime minister. The president, elected by Parliament members for a five-year term, serves as the head of state.

The House's 36 members are elected by the people for five-year terms. Since Trinidad is the more populous island, most House members are Trinidadians, but a rule states that at least two House members must come from Tobago. The president selects the prime minister, who is the leader of the House majority party. The president also appoints the 31 members of the Senate. Senators are chosen using certain guidelines: the president seeks the prime minister's advice for filling 16 positions, confers with the opposition party leader in selecting 6 candidates, and chooses the remaining 9 members using his or her own discretion.

In recent years, Tobago's citizens have expressed a desire for independence from their dominant sister island. As a result, Tobago was granted a 12-member House of Assembly in 1980. The assembly is responsible for administering island government.

The president's residence is surrounded by a neatly sculptured garden.

For 30 years, the majority party in Trinidad and Tobago was the People's National Movement (PNM). However, an opposition party, the National Alliance for Reconstruction (NAR), was formed in the 1980s and ousted the PNM. In turn, the East Indian supporters of the NAR withdrew to form their own party, the United National Congress (UNC), which quickly replaced the NAR as the country's second major political force.

Trinidad is divided, for election purposes, into seven counties and the four largest cities, each administered by elected councils. Tobago forms an eighth county but has some degree of self-government under the Tobago House of Assembly.

The country's legal system is based on British common law. The country's highest court is the Court of Appeals, whose chief justice is chosen by the president with the advice of the prime minister and the opposition leader. However, certain cases can be taken for further appeal to the Privy Council in London.

Public Services

Trinidad and Tobago's national security is protected by the defense force and the police service. The defense force consists of the Regiment, an army battalion with fewer than 1,000 troops, assisted by an even smaller Coast Guard. The 5,300 men and women of the Police Service Department are responsible for internal security. Convicted prisoners are sent to the nation's three prisons: Royal Gaol in Port-of-Spain, Island Prison on Carerra Island, and Grove Prison near Arima.

Islanders receive health care through a system of public hospitals and outpatient health centers. Nurses deliver much of this care, because the nation suffers from a shortage of medical doctors and dentists. The recent development of a national health insurance that provides free medical care is greatly improving the islanders' health. The insurance is also helping to fight poverty through a program of survivor benefits and disability payments.

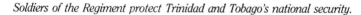

Soldiers of the Regiment protect Trinidad and Tobago's national security.

Since early in the 20th century, Trinidad and Tobago has experienced a rapid and steady population growth. To help keep the population in line with the nation's available resources—housing, jobs, and other necessities—the government sponsors family planning and health-education clinics throughout the cities and countryside. With the help of these clinics, the population growth rate has been brought under control, although poverty remains a major social problem.

Other government programs battle different social problems. For example, undernourished children receive free milk and meals through a government-sponsored school lunch program. The Department of Social Services and Community Development handles many other social services, including help for the needy and programs for juvenile offenders.

Trinidad and Tobago provides free primary, secondary, and technical education. The literacy rate in the islands is 97 percent.

Education

Trinidad and Tobago has greatly improved its educational system in the past few decades. In 1961, only about 51 percent of the population had completed elementary school; 13 percent had never attended school at all. Today, the country provides free primary, secondary, and technical education, and finances part of the cost of attending the local university. The islands can now be proud that 97 percent of the people can read and write.

All children between the ages of 6 and 12 must attend school. At age 12, most students enter the advanced secondary program for six years. Others continue the basic program for two years. Many schools are run by the nation's various religious groups, which receive government funds for education. Two private schools based on the American and Canadian educational system have also been founded.

The nation's only university, the Trinidad branch of the University of the West Indies, is located in Saint Augustine, outside Port-of-Spain. It grants diplomas and advanced degrees in a variety of fields and recently added a school of business. Students who wish to study courses not available on the islands may apply for a government scholarship or financial aid to attend schools abroad. Many islanders have received training and work experience in the United States, Canada, Great Britain, Latin America, Africa, and India.

Over 5,000 students attend several technical and vocational schools, such as the Trinidad and Tobago Hotel School, which teaches hotel administration and service work. The Eric Williams Medical Science Complex opened at Mouth Hope in 1986. The government continues to secure international financing to build new schools and increase the quality of education.

The Point Lisas industrial complex, located off Trinidad's southwest coast, was built by the government to attract heavy industries to the islands.

An Industrial Economy

Trinidad and Tobago once relied primarily on agriculture for income. Today, oil and natural gas together fuel Trinidad and Tobago's economy, accounting for 28 percent of the gross domestic product (GDP) and 22 percent of government revenues. They also provide raw materials for a growing petrochemical industry.

The island's first commercial oil well was sunk in southern Trinidad in 1908. Today, commercial oil operations are found in the southern, eastern, and western ends of the island, and offshore operations have also been established. Oil processing began in 1914 when the first refinery opened. Since then, the nation has gained a reputation as a major oil-refining center. The country houses two of the world's largest refineries, at Point-à-Pierre and Point Fortin. In addition to domestic oil, these refineries process large amounts of imported crude oil from the Middle East, Venezuela, and Indonesia.

The petroleum industry has brought prosperity to Trinidad and Tobago. The country is less dependent on agriculture and has greater economic freedom. Unfortunately, the petroleum industry employs only about 3 percent of the labor force, and most refinery operations are owned and operated by American or British corporations. Therefore, few islanders benefit directly from the industry's profits.

Furthermore, fluctuating oil prices have had a roller-coaster effect on the nation's economy. Although the country is not a member of the Organization of Oil Exporting Countries (OPEC), it experienced sudden profits from OPEC's sharp increase in oil prices in 1973. But when international oil prices plummeted in the 1980s, the nation's crude oil production dropped sharply and economic growth slowed. Production has increased since, but experts predict that the supply will be exhausted by about 2005.

Looking for New Industries

Unemployment is a continuing problem in Trinidad and Tobago. In an effort to combat it, the government has encouraged the development of new industries. Profits from the oil industry have given Trinidad and Tobago's government a chance to help develop other industries. Chief among these is the natural gas industry.

The building of this cement plant brought a new industry—and new jobs—to Trinidad.

With approximately 106 trillion proven natural gas reserves, Trinidad and Tobago is one of the most gas-rich countries in the world. Experts say these reserves could sustain a natural gas industry for another 35 years. The government has taken steps to ensure that the gas is able to reach potential consumers, and natural gas production is increasing steadily. This increase reflects the growing demand for natural gas, as well as its growing supply.

Today, the government is working to attract heavy industry and sophisticated technology that can utilize its natural gas as a fuel and a raw material. One result of this effort is the large industrial complex at Point Lisas, off Trinidad's southwest coast. Natural gas is funneled across the island in an intricate system of government-funded pipelines to be used in ammonia, urea, and steel factories at Point Lisas.

Trinidad and Tobago is one of the world's major producers of ammonia. Two joint ammonia projects operate at Point Lisas and a third at Point Fortin. Great Britain and the United States buy most of the country's ammonia to use in manufacturing fertilizers and other chemicals.

Also located at the Point Lisas industrial complex is the Trinidad and Tobago Methanol Plant. Most of its exported methanol, used as an antifreeze, is shipped to the United States. The complex includes a urea plant as well. The Netherlands, India, and the United States purchase urea, which is used in fertilizers and resins. The Iron and Steel Company of Trinidad and Tobago, also at Point Lisas, produces iron and steel pellets, wire, and rods.

Perhaps Trinidad's oldest industry is asphalt mining from Pitch Lake, near La Brea. It is the world's largest such lake. Natural asphalt has been mined there for about 200 years and sold to countries around the globe. Recently however, sales have declined due to the development of synthetic asphalt.

In recent years, tourism has become an increasingly important industry. Tobago has profited most from this new income source. In addition to international travelers, Tobago attracts Trinidadians who wish to escape to the smaller island on the weekends.

Agriculture

Despite the flurry of industrial growth in Trinidad and Tobago, agricultural exports still play a significant role in the nation's economy. The islands export coconuts, copra (dried coconut meat from which coconut oil can be extracted), cocoa, limes, and livestock. But sugar is still the most important agricultural export. Sugar refineries throughout the islands process sugarcane into molasses and rum for export to countries around the world. The country's sugar production is dominated by major companies that own large, highly mechanized farms. The remaining sugar is grown by about 10,000 peasant farmers, who plow their small tracts of land without modern machinery.

Trinidad and Tobago's second most important crop is cocoa. Other noteworthy exports include citrus fruit, bananas, coffee, rice, coconuts, and copra. Refineries process copra into cooking oil, margarine, and soap.

Despite this tremendous agricultural output, Trinidad and Tobago imports huge amounts of food each year. Traditionally, consumers have preferred the standardized quality and lower prices of imported products (local crops are comparatively expensive because of the high cost of producing them). Meat and dairy items top the list of imported foods.

The Government's Economic Role

Until the late 1980s, the government played the leading role in Trinidad and Tobago's industries, through both ownership of businesses and restrictions on business activities. The government invested directly in petroleum, agriculture, fishing, manufacturing, communications, transport, banking, and tourist industries, and it protected local products by placing tariffs on imported goods.

However, following the widespread collapse of communism in the late 1980s and early 1990s, the United States led a movement to establish free-

Large companies use modern machinery to harvest the valuable sugarcane crop.

market economies and reduce business restrictions. Trinidad responded by selling many holdings to private companies, a process called privatization. This policy has led to an influx of investments by companies from outside the country, especially multinational corporations controlled by the United States and Great Britain.

Income from oil and industrial development has helped raise the islanders' living standard, but there is much room for improvement. The U.S. government's Caribbean Basin Initiative allows the United States to purchase Trinidad and Tobago exports without quotas or duty taxes, and this system has increased trade. The North American Free Trade Agreement is expected to have an even greater impact. Four decades after independence, Trinidad and Tobago has become an economically sound nation.

Wealthy businesspeople once lived in the historic homes surrounding Queen's Park Savannah in Port-of-Spain. Today, most of these houses serve as government buildings.

Bustling Cities, Quiet Villages

Life in Trinidad and Tobago's cities and towns is a contrast of sights, sounds, activities, and lifestyles—ranging from the cosmopolitan excitement of Port-of-Spain, the nation's capital, to the relaxing tranquility of Man O' War Bay, one of the Caribbean's best natural harbors. From Trinidad's Point Lisas Industrial Estate, a hub of noisy economic activity, to the sleepy solitude of Tobago's Charlotteville, a small fishing village located at the island's tip, Trinidad and Tobago combines age-old Caribbean serenity with modern excitement.

Port-of-Spain is the center of all activity in this island nation. It is bounded on one side by one of the Caribbean's busiest harbors and on the other by the 70-acre (28-hectare) Royal Botanical Gardens. The gardens house a wide variety of rare and exotic trees and flowers, including orchids lodged in a special house. Adjoining the botanical gardens is the Emperor Valley Zoo, which features native mammals, birds, and reptiles.

An Olympic-sized stadium and a 200-acre (80-hectare) park are located in the heart of Port-of-Spain. During carnival, Queens Park Savannah becomes the center of activity; come Ash Wednesday, it becomes a quiet park with facilities for soccer, cricket, and horse racing.

Surrounding the park is a unique cluster of ornate buildings from the Victorian period. These houses reflect the diversity of cultural influences

Queens Park Savannah is a quiet recreational center, except during carnival.

found in Trinidad, including Moorish, German, and French. Once the homes of wealthy businessmen, most now serve as government or office buildings. The Jinnah Memorial Mosque, constructed in 1947, provides another insight into this nation's multiethnic society. Named for Mohammad Ali Jinnah, the founder of Pakistan, it is an impressive example of Asian Islamic architecture. The mosque can hold 500 worshipers.

Port-of-Spain's Frederick Street is the hub of urban activity. Stores, boutiques, galleries, restaurants, and street vendors abound. Woodford Square, Independence Square, and Columbus Square are focal points of the downtown area. Also downtown is the National Museum and Art Gallery, once known as the Royal Victoria Institute. Established in 1872, it houses an outstanding collection of carnival costumes, native Indian artifacts, and modern Trinidadian art. The Angostura Bitters Factory, in business since 1824, produces a world-famous bitters (an alcoholic beverage) using a secret recipe. This unusual factory houses a butterfly collection.

A Glimpse of the Past

Located on a 1,100-foot (330-meter) peak overlooking Port-of-Spain is Fort George. Built in 1804, it served as a strategic stronghold and signal station during the wars between England and France. Now restored as a historic monument, it offers a majestic view of the city and harbor.

To the east of Port-of-Spain is Lopinot, a valley nestled between the mountains of the Northern Range. The area offers a view of rural island lifestyle. Located within the valley are the villages of Sirée, La Pastora, and Lopinot, with a combined population of less than 1,000 people.

Many of these villagers are descendants of slaves brought into the valley by the French in the 1800s. According to historians, the Comte de Lopinot marched his slaves up along a river path and established his plantation home amid the lush green surroundings. Today, the government has restored the plantation house and several of the buildings. It also maintains the surrounding natural botanical gardens. Adjoining the area are the Martin Gomez caves.

The Asa Wright Nature Center is located in Arima, about a one-and-a-half hour drive from Port-of-Spain. Situated in the mountains, it is a recreational area and a center for the study of tropical birds and flowers. It features a colony of oilbirds in Dunston Caves—the only oilbird colony in the world that is accessible for scientific study. Arima is also home to Trinidad and Tobago's only surviving American Indians—the Arawaks— and the site of one of the nation's major industrial estates.

The Point Lisas Industrial Estate, covering about 1,600 acres (640 hectares), is situated between Port-of-Spain and San Fernando. The largest industrial complex in the Caribbean, it contains a harbor on the Gulf of Paria, a turning basin, and berthing facilities for loading exports and unloading imports. Housing units in the estate provide accommodations for 20,000 people. Other assets include a large electrical generating station and direct access pipelines to the natural gas fields off Trinidad's southern coast. Fifteen other industrial areas are scattered throughout Trinidad and Tobago. Some of these sites include Point Fortin, Valencia, and Milford on Tobago.

Pitch Lake, near La Brea in southern Trinidad, is the site of asphalt mining. The lake's surface looks like elephant skin and can support a train of railroad mining cars routed over it. Pitch is carved out of this vast field in huge hunks. As the pitch is removed, water fills the holes until more pitch seeps into them, eventually displacing the water and making the pitch supply seem unending. Asphalt from Pitch Lake has been used to pave many streets in the United States.

Tranquil Tobago

Tobago's unspoiled tropical beauty makes it a perfect reprieve from the hustle and bustle of city life. Its scattered villages, pastel-colored houses, small hotels, easygoing people, and relaxed atmosphere reflect the modern-day tranquility of what was once the most-disputed island in the West Indies.

Most of Tobago's population is concentrated in the southern part of the island. More than half of the people reside in the capital and port city of Scarborough. Every morning, Scarborough's central square becomes the site of a lively market, where produce, clothing, livestock, and collectibles are bought, sold, and traded.

The quaintness and serenity of Tobago's small towns attract tourists.

Fort King George offers a glimpse into history and a spectacular ocean view.

Overlooking Scarborough is Fort King George. Built by the British in 1777, the fort was the site of many of the battles for control of Tobago. It was captured by the French in 1781 and renamed Fort Castries, recaptured by the British in 1793, retaken and held by the French from 1802 until 1803, and finally controlled by the British until 1854. Today, the fort provides a wonderful view of the coast on the Atlantic side of the island.

The Mount Irvine Hotel, not far from the airport, has one of the Caribbean's most scenic 18-hole golf courses. The Mount Irvine Bay Hotel ProAm, a golf tournament that attracts professional golfers from around the world, is held here. Off Tobago's southwest coast is the Buccoo Bay Coral Reef Garden, a natural aquarium containing tropical fish and coral. Here snorkelers and scuba divers can swim along with the marine life. At low tide, glass-bottom boats travel to the reef from the village of Buccoo Bay.

Northern Tobago has unspoiled mountains, thick forests, and almost every variety of the island's native wildlife. A winding road runs from the southern part of the island to its northern tip. It passes through cacao fields and sugar and coconut plantations. Two of Tobago's best beaches are at Store Bay in the south and Man O' War Bay in the north.

Since 1970, the islands' transportation and communications systems have greatly improved. Minibuses called maxi-taxis are a form of public transportation.

Transportation and Communications

The Republic of Trinidad and Tobago has been working steadily to update its transportation and communications systems to meet the growing demand for better service. Road construction still does not meet the needs of the population, and experts say the road system may not be adequate for a few years. Telephone service, however, has been upgraded significantly, especially for international calls.

By the mid-1990s, about 150,000 vehicles plied the nation's roads, or roughly one for every eight inhabitants. Although Trinidad and Tobago's 4,750 miles (7,600 kilometers) of roads reach nearly every corner of the country, many rural roads are no more than single-lane dirt paths. In the cities, where roads tend to be better, traffic jams are common.

About 2,500 miles (4,000 kilometers) of road are paved. Modern, two-lane highways span the lengths of both islands. One of Trinidad's most important road improvements has been the conversion of an outdated rail line into a transit route for buses. This provides more efficient transportation from the east-west corridor to the major industrial cities. Other noteworthy progress includes the widening of existing highways to accommodate two-way traffic, the construction of new secondary roads, and the improvement of existing secondary roads. On Tobago, the recently completed Claude Noël Highway (named after an award-winning sportsman) skirts around Scarborough. Nevertheless, travel throughout Tobago is slow, regardless of road quality or size. To maintain the island's tranquility, island officials enforce a 30-mile- (48-kilometer-) per-hour speed limit.

Both islands have public transportation. The government-owned Public Service Corporation provides bus service throughout the islands. This service is inexpensive, but rarely sticks to schedules. Privately owned taxis, route taxis, and maxi-taxis (similar to minibuses) offer other alternatives. Route taxis and maxi-taxis follow specific courses, picking up and discharging passengers along the way. They are found all over the islands, and passengers can hail them with a hand signal.

Small craft known as "Down-the-Islands" boats ferry passengers among Trinidad and Tobago and the surrounding islands.

Trinidad and Tobago has nine harbors—eight in Trinidad and one in Tobago. Many European and North American shipping lines use Trinidad as a port of call. Port-of-Spain is the major port. It is used mainly for the import and export of cargo and refrigerated goods, but also serves as a bunking port for ships traveling between North and South America. Trinidad and Tobago's other large ports are Point Lisas and Scarborough.

The nation has no large inland waterways for carrying cargo or passengers within the islands. However, ferries provide service between the islands. Ferries leave from Saint Vincent's Pier in Port-of-Spain and arrive in Scarborough about six hours later.

Traditionally, the government played a major role in regional and domestic shipping, but here, as elsewhere in the economy, control is passing into the hands of private corporations. A large number of private shipping agents have set up shop in Trinidad and Tobago to oversee and direct the increasing sea traffic.

Piarco International Airport, one of the largest and busiest airports in the Caribbean, sits about 13 miles (21 kilometers) southeast of Port-of-Spain. It accommodates the regularly scheduled flights of most major airlines and serves as the home of British West Indian Air (BWIA), the national airline. The government has developed a 25-year plan to improve Piarco to include a new terminal, expanded cargo facilities, hotels, and an industrial park.

The Air Caribbean domestic service shuttles passengers between Piarco and Crown Point Airport, located on Tobago's southwestern tip. In addition, small planes hop between the country's four smaller airports and various Caribbean islands.

Communications

Two major newspapers are published in Trinidad and Tobago, the conservative *Trinidad Guardian* and the more sensational *Trinidad Express*. The *Express* has a few more readers than the *Guardian*. Other news publications include the *Evening News*, the *Sun*, the biweekly *Trinidad and Tobago Mirror*, and several weekly papers.

The country is served by two AM radio stations and nine FM bands, with a full range of programming. One government-owned television station transmits programs to the approximately 400,000 television sets in the country. Operating on five channels, it offers programs such as feature films, community interest shows, news and information programs, shows geared to children and teens, and dramas. In addition, Trinidadians can receive close to 40 cable TV channels. About half of all television programming comes from other countries, especially the United States, Canada, Australia, and Germany.

The country has only one television station; the government owns and operates it.

Domestic telephone service, once notoriously slow and unreliable, has improved dramatically. International calling is modern and efficient, with state-of-the-art communications equipment. Trinidad and Tobago has also developed a strong presence on the Internet, where the government provides extensive business and tourist information on the World Wide Web. Many large businesses maintain Web sites, as do several schools.

Trinidad's future seems bright. Its young people are well educated, yet retain a respect for the traditions that make their islands unique.

A Promising Land

The Republic of Trinidad and Tobago has successfully adapted to the many changes it has endured throughout its history. Columbus's discovery of Trinidad in 1498 and Britain's claim over Tobago in 1608 led the way for European settlement. The settlers eventually overcame the native Arawak and Carib populations and, after initial disappointment in the islands' lack of precious metals, found that the islands were valuable in other ways.

As Caribbean trade and exploration grew, Trinidad and Tobago became important for their strategic locations along trade routes. Settlers also found the fertile valleys would grow profitable tobacco, sugarcane, and cacao crops. The Europeans introduced African slaves, then Asian indentured servants, to work the plantations, paving the way for the ethnic mix that exists today.

After Britain finally won the islands (Trinidad in 1802 and Tobago in 1814), it combined them into one colony and built government and legal systems based on British example. The islands' culture grew to reflect native and well as outside influences. For example, while the islanders enjoyed British sports, they created their own musical styles with calypso and steel bands. Economically, the islands moved from the agricultural system of the 1700s and 1800s into the industrial 1900s by developing a petroleum industry.

Trinidad and Tobago obtained limited self-government in 1956 and independence in 1962. It finally broke ties with England by becoming a republic in 1976. As the government worked to bring education, transportation, and communications up to modem standards, it was also faced with a high unemployment rate and a decline in oil prices, which brought on a recession lasting from the late 1980s well into the 1990s.

The country has dealt successfully with many of these problems. Attempts to lure investment to the country, including the privatization of industry, have brought economic growth. Trinidad and Tobago now boasts excellent airports, seaports, and communications systems, and its financial services tie it firmly into the Latin American economy. The oil in the country's reserves may not last much longer, but natural gas is taking its place as a leading source of both energy and trade income.

A major exception to the nation's success is its chronic unemployment, which worsens as the population shifts from rural to urban. Poverty and housing shortages plague the cities. Since many of the newer industries depend more on technology than on human labor, a long-range solution to unemployment remains unclear.

Politically, despite a failed coup attempt by militants in 1990, the islands enjoy a stable government, and the major parties share common goals: increased industrialization, upgraded communications and transportation systems, and redistribution of wealth from the white aristocracy to the black and East Indian majority.

The population mix of African, East Indian, and European peoples provides a dynamic culture. The terrain, plants, and animals are equally diverse. And the two sister islands, one bustling and cosmopolitan, the other more tranquil, complement each other remarkably well. Trinidad and Tobago appears poised for a prosperous and expansive future.

◄GLOSSARY►

Accra Seasoned fish cakes served with fritters.

American Indians These peoples, sometimes called Amerindians, are descended from Mongoloid stock and are the original inhabitants of the Western Hemisphere.

Archipelago A chain of islands that are all part of the same under-sea mountain formation.

Calypso A rhythmic form of song that originated in Trinidad and Tobago, with lyrics that often comment on society.

Caribbean shirt jac A belted jacket and scarf worn by many men in the capital city of Port-of-Spain.

Carnival A lavish festival, featuring costumes, parades, and contests, that is held every year before the beginning of Lent.

Courtlanders People from Latvia on the Baltic Sea. Many Court-landers settled on Tobago during the 17th century.

Creoles People of mixed African and European descent.

Dimanche Gras The Sunday before Ash Wednesday, marked by festivals and parties.

Indentured servant A person contracted to work for a specified period of time.

Pans A general term for the instruments of a steel band.

Petit carême The short, dry spell occurring during September and October.

Pitch lake   A lake containing natural tar. The world's largest pitch lake is located on Trinidad.

Roti   Thin pancakes stuffed with curried meat and/or vegetables.

Sans couche   A stew of beef, pig's tail, onions, and seasonings served with dumplings.

Steel band   A group of musical instruments created in Trinidad that are made from oil drums. Also, the type of music played by the musicians.

◄ I N D E X ►

ACKNOWLEDGMENTS

AP/Wide World Photos (p. 56); Maggie Berkvist (pp. 2, 14, 20, 36, 41, 42a, 42b, 43a, 46a, 47a, 48a, 48b, 72, 73, 74, 76–77, 79, 80); Division of Information, Office of the Prime Minister (pp. 16, 21, 32, 33, 38, 39, 62, 64, 67); Len Kaufman (pp. 43b, 44–45, 45b, 46b, 47b, 50, 70); Norton Studios Ltd. (pp. 43c, 46c, 51); Paria Publishing Co. Ltd. (pp. 26, 29, 31); TIDCO (p. 60); Trinidad and Tobago Tourist Board (pp. 18, 23, 25, 44a, 44b, 45a, 48, 53, 55, 58, 59, 68); UPI/Bettmann Newphotos (p. 34). Photo Research: Maggie Berkvist.